A *Shattered* Family

Denise Dove-Bernier

PAGE PUBLISHING, INC.
Conneaut Lake, PA

First originally published by Page Publishing 2019

ISBN 978-1-64584-910-0 (pbk)
ISBN 978-1-64584-911-7 (digital)

Printed in the United States of America

IN LOVING MEMORY

I wish you were still here,
Momma, to see this book come out.
You always were so very proud, like
You wanted to be Momma.

But I know that you are looking on in the cloud of witnesses.

Therefore, since we are surrounded by such a great cloud of witnesses, let us throw off everything that hinders and the sin that so easily entangles, and let us run with perseverance the race marked out for us.

Also, this book is dedicated to my two big brothers, Wayne and Doug, and my daddy, Miss you all so much!

Mary Watson
May 17, 1944–December 18, 2018

Henry Babin Jr.
December 7, 1939–July 27, 1994

Wayne Watson Jr.
June 8, 1963–November 9, 1986

Doug Watson
March 15, 1965–October 17, 2017

INTRODUCTION

Father God let me know that the reason for allowing me all the alone time is so I could write my book. Oh my gosh, when I heard this from Father God, I thought this is deep. I find that telling my story takes a lot of strength and courage. When I started writing this book, it felt like I was reliving all the pain I went through with the divorce. Also, when writing this book, I told God, "This book was Your idea, so God, You need to help me with it."

Just for the record, this book is not to get back at my ex. This is not a revenge thing; the Lord let me know it's for "inner healing" since I've been in Connecticut.

I was in a hurry to receive my healing, and Father God let me know that it is a process.

—Dee

ACKNOWLEDGMENTS

I want to give a very special thanks to the people who encouraged me to write this book and tell my story, "my personal testimony." First and foremost, I want to give a huge shout-out to my beautiful Savior, Jesus Christ. Without my Father God's help, I could do absolutely nothing! I want to thank Him first for having the people that He gave me, to help encourage and support me through my writings.

The people that Father God blessed me in my life with. I want to thank you all so very much, for all of your love and support. I couldn't have pressed on without all of your encouragement; I love you all so very much.

I also want to say that I have forgiven my ex-husband and the woman that he is now married to. Even though it broke my heart and broke me, it seemed, at the time, into *a million* pieces, and ended up scattering the children and hurting them through it, which I hated how it hurt them though. If it did not happen, I wouldn't have learned all I've learned about how it is when Christians have to face a divorce they never want to face. Even though it was wrong and a sin, it propelled me *deeper* in my personal relationship with Jesus. Also, it enabled me to touch the lives of those hurt in the Christian community and non-Christian community (the unbelievers), who have been hurt and devastated by the effects of divorce.

Also, if it did not happen, my now wonderful, God-fearing husband, Rob, would not be in my life. So I don't believe in coincidence, luck, or accidents. Father God knew everything that was going to happen. But, that doesn't mean that Father God does not give us choices in this life, we are not robots as I have stated time and time again. We have a choice of blessings—the Word says or curses. He said for us to choose life though.

So know this, the choices and decisions you make in your lives don't just affect you, they affect everyone, they affect your children, and also, they affect the kingdom of God, the body of Christ. But thank you, because now I am now a better Christian woman, better minister and servant of the Gospel of Jesus Christ.

> This day, I call the heavens and the earth as witnesses against you that I have set before your life and death, blessings, and curses. Now choose life so that you and your children may live. (Deuteronomy 30:19)

Thank you,

Mary Jane Watson (Momma)
Ismah Pratt (aunt)
Rob Bernier (my loving, God-fearing husband)
Wayne McGeathy (son)
Matthew Watson (son)
Liliana Dove (daughter)
Luke Dove (son)
Heaven Dove (daughter)
Kimberly Truscott (sister)
Donnetta Hulin (sister)
Doug Watson (brother)
Henry Babin, Jr. (Daddy)
Jana Berger (sister)
Angela Dore (sister)
Yvonne Dore (sister)
Richard Shock (uncle)
Doris Covington (aunt)
Shirley Fee (aunt)
Alanah (first granddaughter).

And, if a woman has a husband who is not a believer, and he is willing to live with her, she must not divorce him. For the unbelieving husband has been sanctified through his wife, and the unbelieving wife has been sanctified through her believing husband. Otherwise, your children would be unclean, but as it is, they are holy. (1 Corinthians 7:13–14)

CHAPTER ONE

The Fall of a Family

It was February of 2015. I didn't know it, but the fate of my family would soon be changed forever. I was waiting for my spouse to come home, because we had reservations for a nice restaurant to celebrate our fourteenth wedding anniversary. But he never came home that night. I was waiting at my mother's house all day for his phone call, but he never called. I remember how heartbroken I was. I told my mom that I would wait until the very last minute to call and cancel our reservations.

My spouse was missing for about seventy-two hours. So a friend of the family came over to comfort me and the kids. She bought pizza for me and the children that night. She had to convince me to call the police, to file a missing-person report on him. The police woman asked me if I thought that my husband was having an affair. I looked at her, very shocked and surprised that she would ask me that. I was very appalled at that question being asked, because I was worried sick and so were the children, thinking that something horrible might have happened to my husband. I told her, "No, there's no way he would do that!"

Anyways, I ended up doing a missing-person report.

The kids and I were very distraught thinking that something horrible did, indeed, happen to him. The friend of the family helped plaster our renewal of vows, wedding photos all over the internet, and the story went viral. People I didn't even know were sharing the post all over the country. There was many people praying he would have been found safe. When the truth came out later where he really was, people were angry about it, because everyone, including me and the kids, were so upset.

On the day, he showed up at the house. My cell phone rang. I answered it. He said that he was at the house. I almost got into a car accident, because I drove home so fast. When I got there, I jumped out of my truck and ran to him, throwing my arms around him and hugging him tight. I said to him, "Thank You, Jesus, that you're alive!" We went into the house, he walked past our pictures on the living room wall.

He cried as he walked past the pictures. Then he said, "I'm not good enough for you and these kids."

I was confused about him crying. Then I asked him, "Why are you crying? Me and the kids have been worried sick about you, thinking you were murdered or something."

He had to go talk to his boss, whom he worked for when he got home, he said. So I told him that I would go in there when he talked to his boss. He kept insisting that I wait in the truck with the children. I told him, "There's no way I'm waiting outside. I'm going in there with you."

When we went inside, his boss started lecturing him about marriage. His boss said he'd like to see us work out the marriage. My ex turned white as a ghost as he sat there with his "Christian" boss laying the marriage lecturing on thick.

His bosses church was having a "couple dance" for marriage's. His boss let us know about it. He said he'd love to see us go. I really wanted to go; my eyes lighted up when his boss mentioned it. My spouse said he'd think about it.

The day he decided to show back up, there was a man in the area that contacted me, and was going to help me do a manhunt for my spouse. He said, "I won't quit or give up until he's found." Also, I was getting ready that day to contact the local news stations back, because they were going to broadcast and be interviewed.

In about three days later, he went away for the weekend. He said that he had "a side job" to do so that we'd have extra money—from which, of course, like always, I never saw any money. He said he was earning for the family. I always believed everything he said, like the good Christian trusting wife was supposed to do, or so I believed.

My oldest daughter had a girlfriend stay the night, like she usually did. The two youngest kids were downstairs playing together around the house as usual. My oldest daughter yelled upstairs to my bedroom, "I think Dad's cheating on you!"

I got upset with her and told her, "No, he's not. That's ridiculous." I didn't believe it or want to hear that, so I kept tuning her out while cleaning my bedroom. I always seemed to stick up for my ex-husband.

My oldest son, Wayne, would get so mad, because he said I'd say, "That's my husband, don't talk about my husband." I had rose-colored glasses on when it came to him, blinders on, if you will. What it was is that I wanted everything to be fine, and I figured if I said it, it would become fine. But, obviously, everyone knows that is not what happened to my marriage.

My ex-husband would go away every single weekend. It was his new habit, which he started in January, it seemed, for the new year. He was always saying he was just trying to make some extra money for the family because we needed it.

When the weekend came again, he took his work boots and walked out the front door, down the side walk. He was smiling as he walked away, with his work boots in his hands. Our two-year-old daughter crying for him as he left. I tried to reassure the baby that "Daddy is leaving for work." I kept saying to her over and over again, but it did not comfort her because she cried even harder.

> For there is nothing hidden that will not be disclosed, and nothing concealed that will not be known or brought out into the open. (Luke 8:17, NIV)

For nothing is secret that shall not be made manifest.

Neither anything hid that shall not be known and come abroad. (Luke 8:17, KJV)

CHAPTER TWO

The Night That Would Forever Change Our Lives

I went upstairs to clean up our bedroom. I heard the voice of God, that still small voice. He told me to go through my husband's bedroom dresser drawers, which, I wasn't the wife that invaded my husband's privacy, ever in all the years of the marriage. So I started to go through the dresser. I said out loud, "Lord, this is crazy. I don't know what I am supposed to be looking for." Then, I lifted up a pair of jeans. I stumbled upon a cell phone.

I then heard the voice of God again, "Now, turn it on and look." Then I saw a conversation pop up right away. I then knew about the affair that my husband hid so well from me. It took me about an hour to read the whole dialogue between him and the woman. I read the whole thing to my sister in Louisiana, crying hysterically throughout the whole thing in major disbelief.

When I had gotten off the phone with her, I started screaming, wailing, crying at the top of my lungs, like I have never done before in my life, not like that. The intense pain, and the flood of a whole bunch of intense emotions flooded my being. I was in major, intense shock, it was more than my heart, mind, and spirit could handle. All the emotions came out all at once. Rage, unbearable sadness, disappointment, pain, loss, abandonment, bitterness, anger, confusion, anxiety, anguish, loneliness, betrayal, helplessness, distrust, rejection, fear, resentment, and dread.

The presence of God was with me in the bedroom, and the presence of the enemy (Satan) was there. I definitely could feel that there were some evil spirits in there with me. With a house full of young children downstairs, I almost did the unthinkable. I fought so hard not to pick up my husband's gun and put it to my head. I felt that I was struggling with an unseen force that was so intense, at that very moment, with me in that room. I was definitely aware of it, because I was no stranger to the unseen realm.

> For our struggle is not against flesh and blood.,
> but against the rulers., against the powers of this
> dark world and against the spiritual forces of evil
> in the heavenly realms. (Ephesians 6:12)

I believe the power of God was so strong that Father God kept me from ending my life that night.

My older daughter and her friend were so distraught when they heard me screaming and heard me talk about killing myself. My daughter then called my pastor's wife and told her, "My mom's talking about killing herself with a gun."

My pastor and his wife were in my house in about five minutes, they rushed there. I heard my pastor's wife at my bathroom door. "Denise" is all she said as I was crying hysterically and wailing uncontrollably behind the bathroom door.

After I knew what the truth was, of what my spouse was doing, I was absolutely devasted! I would cry myself to sleep every single night, with chest pains and severe emotional pain for a month and a half. My baby, Heaven, the youngest, slept right on top of me for two weeks straight. I would try put her on the side of me, and she would get right back on my chest.

My mother and my oldest son were so worried about me, that after the first month, they had me come over there and stay on my mom's couch for about three weeks when everything was still fresh.

I drove my oldest son nuts because I would cry and mention my ex-spouse's name over and over again, every single day, most of the day off and on.

Thank You, Father God, for all the pain I been through, for molding me and using my pain to touch others in pain.

—Dee

I think my son was embarrassed to go around with me in public because I couldn't control my emotions. I would break down crying in public. I broke down crying at the pizza shop, and the guy behind the counter had to come out and give me a hug. Also, one day, I hug my mom and just cried in her arms like a baby.

When I finally went back home to my house, I went and got every single picture or memory of my marriage, and quickly as I could, I boxed and bagged them up. I took it all over to my mother's house. I made sure that I didn't destroy any of them because that was the kids' dad. Also, I downsized all my things in the whole house, from top to bottom. Got rid of anything of negative energy, especially if it had any memories of my ex-spouse.

My two teenagers actually knew about my husband's affair way before I knew anything, because he told them about the woman. He was showing pictures of her to them, wanting to know what they thought about her. My teenage son told me that he overheard him on the phone with another woman, and he said that he knew that was not Mom. The kids didn't know how to tell their mom, they told me. Also, that should have never been put on them, two teenagers, in the first place.

I thought I was going to die from a broken heart.

—Dee

CHAPTER THREE

Dreams Shattered

I ended up having an emergency hernia surgery in early April of 2015. It was very difficult having a toddler little girl and a little boy that was five years old, along with my two teen kids, having to have that surgery. My youngest ended up getting out of the house because I was drugged up on my pain medicine and passed out on my couch in the living room. So I ended up having some neighbors down the street from us call CPS on me, thinking that I was just neglecting my children, not looking after them.

There was a night that that woman had left him because they had a fight. I guess my ex-husband texted me and told me, "Do you ever miss me?"

I quickly changed the subject! I told him that I was doing okay.

Then he said, "Well, I miss you, and I'm glad you're doing okay."

This conversation happened in December of 2015. I thought to myself, *There is no way that I am going to say that I missed him.*

During the month of April of 2015, I asked my spouse at the time if he had gone and filed divorce papers. He said, yelling in my face, "Is that what you want?"

I was standing in the kitchen crying, which didn't mean anything to him. I thought to myself, *That was always my dream, to have my husband commit adultery.*

My ex-husband did let me know before he was over, in person, that he didn't want counseling or want to talk to a pastor either. He said he made his choice and that he would live with it. My ex avoided me when it came to serving him the divorce papers. I had to contact the woman he was with and say, "Could you please bring him to the courthouse so I can have my divorce." Which, I am forever grateful to her that she made sure he went.

When he first got served at my lawyer's office, my sister in Michigan went with me for moral support But the first court date he missed, he said he wasn't able to make it. The day of the divorce on the other court date, on February 29, 2016, two good friends went with me. One was a friend from church, and the other was a friend from my college.

My two friends said I looked so happy that day, like a school girl. But they said, "He, however, wasn't looking as happy." I drove around the courthouse building, beeping my horn on my truck and waving! I was thinking, *I'm finally set free from an abusive marriage!*

I was given some godly counsel and advice while going through my divorce. They told me that I had to go through it, not over it, not around it, definitely no putting some of it under the rug. But I had to go through it, the emotions and pain of the divorce.

> But now, this is what the Lord says, "He who created you, Jacob, He who formed you, Israel."
>
> "Do not fear, for I have redeemed you; I have summoned you by name; you are Mine. When you pass through the waters, I will be with you; and when you pass through the fire, you will not be burned; the flames will not set you ablaze.
>
> For I am the Lord, your God, the Holy One of Israel, your savior; I give Egypt for your ransom, Cush and Seba, in your stead. Since you are precious and honored in my sight, and because I love you, I will give in exchange for you, nations in exchange for your life. Do not be afraid for I am with you; I will bring your children from the west.

I will say to the north, "'Give them up!' and to the south, 'Do not hold them back.' Bring my sons from afar and my daughters from the ends of the earth—everyone who is called by My name, whom I created for My glory, whom I formed and made."

Lead out those who have eyes but are blind, who have ears but are deaf. All the nations gather together, and the peoples assemble. Which of their gods foretold this and proclaimed to us the former things? "Let them bring in their witnesses," declares the Lord, "and My servant, whom I have chosen so that you may know and believe Me and understand that I am He. Before Me, no god was formed, nor will there be one after Me.

I, even I, am the Lord, and apart from Me, there is no savior. I have revealed and saved and proclaimed I, and not some foreign god among you. "You are My witnesses," declares the Lord, "that I am God. Yes, and from ancient days, I am He. No one can deliver out of MY hand. When I act, who can reverse it? (Isaiah 43:1–13)

My *momentary* pain will be worth it, all one day to see others set free and ministered to by my "personal testimony."

—Dee

The reason I wanted to not go through it fully, the emotions of it, was because it was very painful. I just wanted it to be over quickly (the divorce). Father God had me go through it because it was the only way that I would heal completely, by working through the emotions instead of suppressing my emotions, which would cause more problems later on if I didn't experience the emotions of going through my divorce.

Divorce, I have to say from my own experience, like many people have before me, is definitely very much like going through a death of losing a loved one in your life. In fact, it is I who find such a "spiritual darkness." One of the things I learned from the divorce is that everyone goes through divorce differently. Like a death of a loved one, everyone goes through that differently. Some people hurt more than others do. I learned by going through the divorce. For one, now I'll be able to relate and help minister to others. I do believe that is why we go through some of our even most painful trails in our life. God uses the experiences of our pain to help comfort others with the same comfort we have received while going through our own personal pain. But the little girl inside Denise, "little Dee Dee" inside of her spirit man was screaming, "No, no more pain." I didn't want to go through no more pain.

It makes me think of when our Lord Jesus at Gethsemane, when He was praying, He said, "My Father, if it is possible, may this cup be taken from Me. Yet, not as I will, but as you will" (Matthew 26:39).

> I consider that our present sufferings are not worth comparing with the glory that will be revealed in us. (Romans 8:18)

I feel like I was forced into the divorce, because what choice did I have when my spouse was already shacked up to another woman in another country. When I was going through the divorce, it also made me look back at the marriage, making me think how "used and abused" I was. I was believing and hoping for God to do a miracle and heal and restore my marriage. God did end up doing a miracle, just not the one I expected.

When 2015 hit, I had no idea or clue of what was ahead of me. But I want to say this, "Nothing that has happened or is ahead of us takes Father God by surprise." Sometimes one of the people in a marriage put one hundred percent of their selves in, but it doesn't work if the other spouse is not doing likewise. It takes three to make a marriage work. It takes God, the husband, and the wife. If you both don't have a heart after God, it is really hard to work things out then. Sometimes, you may not realize or be in denial that you had been unequally yoked.

> Do not be yoked together with unbelievers. For what do righteousness and wickedness have in common? Or what fellowship can light have with darkness? (2 Corinthians 6:14)

This book is also part of my "inner healing."

—Dee

I thought I was done with being broken, until 2015 hit. Then, it was such a realization to me that "Dee, as long as you are in this fallen world, and as long as you are, you are in your fragile body, you may be broken again."

Jesus said, "Count it all joy when you go through trails of many kinds. In this world, you will have trouble, but don't be discouraged, because I have overcome the world" (John 16:33).

> You intended to harm me but God intended it
> for good, to accomplish what is now being done,
> the saving of many, many lives. (Genesis 50:20)

> God is always up to doing a new thing He said in
> His Word. See, I am doing a new thing! Now it
> springs up; do you not perceive it? I am making a
> way in the wilderness. (Isaiah 43:19)

He has been continuing to renew me from the inside out. I may have been broken in 2015, and I thought was beyond repair and healing, but that ended up not being true, that I could never be healed and repaired—my heart, soul (emotions), and spirit. I was broken, but now, I am even more beautiful inside and outside than ever before. I had my own personal doubts that I could move on and keep living life and be completely healed from the enormous pain from a divorce.

But Father God showed me different. He showed me that I could because of Him. He showed me that I just needed to trust Him with helping me through the emotional pain of a divorce. Satan stripped me of a lot of things in my life. But Father God is in the business of restoring everything that the devil has stolen. He promises in His Word to restore the years the locust have eaten.

I will repay you for the years the locusts have
eaten—the great locust and the young locusts
and the locust swarm—My great army that I sent
among you. (Joel 2:25)

The devil thought that, by him destroying my marriage and
family, he would successfully destroy me.

Healing is like an onion: there are many layers that need to be peeled away, until you get to the root of the core.

—Dee

The Lord is close to the broken hearted and saves who are crushed in spirit. (Psalm 34:18)

CHAPTER FOUR

Coming Out of the Ashes

Father God took me out of my abusive marriage. If it would have been left up to me, I would have been in it another twenty years or more. Because for one, I am the type of person who never gives up on anything, and especially a marriage. I didn't realize that I needed to be set free from the marriage I worked so hard to hold together. I know that it is Father God Who (actually) is the glue that holds marriages together. In our own effort, we can do nothing, and when we think we can, then that's where pride comes in and the Word of God says that "Pride comes before a fall."

> Pride goes before destruction, a haughty spirit before a fall. (Proverbs 16:18)

> "Not by might nor by power, but by My Spirit," says the Lord Almighty. (Zechariah 4:6)

> So if you think you are standing firm, be careful not to fall! (1 Corinthians 10:12)

When everyone found out the truth of where my spouse was after he had been reported as "a missing person," I thought to myself, *I have never been so embarrassed and humiliated in my life.* My ex-spouse was running around with many, many women throughout our entire marriage. Also, I was not the first wife he had done that too.

From what I gather, he had been married several times, I guess before me, and had kids all over the place. But I was the woman who was with him the longest and had the most children with him. I always believed him when he told me that it was always his ex-wives' fault and not his, about his previous divorces. People often asked me what part I played in the breakup of my marriage. The only conclusion I can come to is, "I was too gullible and believed everything he told me."

> He heals the brokenhearted and binds up their
> wounds. (Psalm 147:3)

CHAPTER FIVE

Anger: The Dark Side of Emotions of a Divorce

Every so often, anger would rise up in me. I learned that anger is also part of the grieving process. Anger was talked about at the Christian Divorce Care Group. I was always faithful and loyal. I wondered why—why, God, why? I have been through pain and been hurt my whole life. It felt like my heart was physically hurt. There was actually a lot of pain coming and going in my chest.

Did my best to fight the depression off, because the depression had me feeling pain and aches all over my body. If it weren't for my personal relationship with Jesus Christ, I would have, definitely, given up. He held and sustained me and the kids. I was surprised at myself with all the anger and rage that came out of inside me. The pain I felt was unbearable at times; I was no stranger to pain. Also, I have learned that our wonderful Father God, though, "never wastes a hurt."

My emotions going through the divorce was like a roller coaster. I didn't know that I could get that angry. I felt so bad, because I took out my anger mostly on my two teenage children during my divorce. They would bring their teen friends over the house all the time, and their friends would disrespect me. So I found myself doing a lot of yelling and screaming. My blood pressure, I'm sure, went through the roof.

I think that it got to be overwhelming for me. I was clearly angered over everything being dumped on me—the house, the bills, and too many. The pressure of being a single mother, which I never had dreamed would happen to me after being married all those years. Which, all of what I was going through was considered "the norm" for someone who was going through an unexpected divorce.

Feeling and experiencing the emotions of anger, I find was so hard on me, being a Christian woman and all. But I realized just because I was a Christian woman, I was also still *very human*. It was okay to go through my emotions and feel every single one of them. As long as I kept giving it all to Father God on a daily continual basis. I felt Satan was getting a foothold sometimes because there were many instances where I could not control my anger. Sometimes, in fact, definitely, my anger would get the best of me. I felt like "a devil" when I got angry. The anger seemed so intense that I didn't know what to do with it. It lasted for quite a few months—the anger I had felt during my divorce. The emotion of anger, in fact, was right after the crying spells. It was the second emotion that I went through, it felt just horrible, just horrible, especially being a Christian woman with a major call of God on my life. Father God kept whispering to me, "Denise, it's okay, give all of these anger emotions to Me."

He, who the Son sets free is free indeed.

(John 8:36)

The other woman texted me just before the court date for the divorce, saying, "I thought this was finally my time to be happy."

—Dee

Father God set me free from the marriage I was in. I had no idea that I needed to be set free from it. I had the belief (conviction) that "marriage" is for life. It was against my belief to have a divorce, because, also, Father God hates divorce.

> For I hate divorce," says the Lord, the God of Israel, "and him who covers his garment with wrong," says the Lord of hosts. "So, take heed to your spirit, that you do not deal treacherously . . . (Bible Gateway)

I mean, after all, since I was a Christian woman, I needed to realize that divorce happens to Christians and non-Christians. The Bible says that "It rains on the just and the unjust."

> That ye may be the children of your Father who is in heaven. For He maketh His sun to rise on the evil and on the just and on the unjust. (Matthew 5:45)

I was a huge "faith woman." I was always praying for God to heal my husband and mend the marriage. I would speak the Word of God over our family and marriage. Now, as I look back at my entire marriage, for me, I can honestly say that I am happy all of it happened, because it made me a better person. It needed to happen, to change me for the better. Also, so I could help minister to other Christians and even the non-Christians who have been hurt and devasted by divorce. I firmly believe that.

This is not the end of our lives, just new beginnings. It is a stepping stone to better and bigger things in life. You can learn some things from it—it can either break you or make you. You can either become bitter, or you can become better, for not letting it destroy or define you. I learned from one of my old pastor's in Michigan that "Marriage in itself is perfect. God made and ordained it. It is people who have problems not marriage, because marriage is beautifully made by Father God, the Creator of the Universe." It is people who are not perfect for sure.

My pastor in Michigan used to say that "There's no perfect churches, and that the minute you and I walked into the church, then the church became imperfect." Because we are all imperfect people with our own individual flaws and imperfections. But, we believers serve a perfect God who sees all, and is willing and able to help us in our imperfections, flaws, weaknesses, and our temptations, and all. But that's, of course, if—and I mean a big *if*—we give everything over to the care of our Father God. We weren't meant to deal with and handle all of our problems, including marriage problems, ect., and the list can go on and on; we were designed to have an *inner* need of God in all of our lives. A hole inside of us that is empty, and we are supposed to be letting Father God fill that empty hole—that void we have in each and every one of us.

If we could handle marriage, and all the many, many areas of our lives on our own, then, we wouldn't need Jesus; we wouldn't need a savior, would we? He just wants us all to have a deep, intimate personal relationship with each one of us. That is definitely *the Gospel truth*. So, my friend, make sure you turn all of your cares of this life over to the care of our loving Father God, because there is no one who loves you as deeply as Father God does.

I had to stop myself from continuing to love a man that continually would misuse and abuse me.

—Dee

CHAPTER SIX

Being Unequally Yoked

I have looked back at my marriage, and I remember a pastor at one of my old churches warned me not to marry him. But I believed different, so I went ahead and married him. My pastor at the time said, "Because you and him might have fun together, but you two will never connect spiritually." Sometimes, I sure do wish I would have listened to the man of God that Father God was trying to speak to me through back then, when I think back.

> Do not be yoked together with unbelievers. For what do righteousness and wickedness have in common? Or what fellowship can light have with darkness? (2 Corinthians 6:14)

If both spouses submit to God, then there is hope. The way I look at my past marriage now is "I didn't need to be spending the rest of my remaining life with a man who didn't genuinely love me." I didn't need to continue to live *a lie*. However, my children are the "only good" that came out of my marriage. Me and my ex-husband first got married on February 16, 2001. We, then later, renewed our vows on August 17, 2013.

One time, I was sick at home, and I couldn't go to church with my ex-husband and the kids. My ex-husband forgot to bring his Bible to church; they asked him, "Where is your Bible at?"

He said, "It's at home, it's my wife."

He called me a "walking Bible." Which today, when I think back on that, I take it as a huge compliment. Also, me and my ex-husband had a prophesy about me and him speaking to other couple's about marriage in arenas filled with thousands of people. We were laying hands on these couples, their marriages would be healed, marriages Satan thought he had. We would not be charging, and other couples would bless our lives. This is on a CD given to us a week before we renewed our vows on August 17, 2013.

Also, I never did get to put my renewed of vows wedding pictures on my living room walls. The renewal of vow wedding was my "big dream wedding," just not with the right man, little did I know that though. I had all my close family and friends there and in it.

My mother said, "If we would have known how he really was, then we could have saved all the money we spent for the wedding for my divorce instead!"

We had one of my cousin's photograph the entire wedding and the reception. The DJ was the minister, and he videotaped the whole thing. All five of our children were in the wedding. My momma was there in her wheelchair.

Father God is never gonna give you someone else's spouse.

—Dee

My mother had eye surgery done so that she would be able to see and enjoy the wedding because none of my family members were there when we first had gotten married on February 16, 2001. There was a lot of "financial abuse" throughout the marriage. I had no idea or gave "financial abuse" much thought. He would throw a fit about even paying one bill, like the water bill, for instance. He would expect me to cover the majority of the bills on mine and my son's fixed income throughout the marriage. He would pocket his own money to do as he wished, which now later, I understand it was so he could run around with all the women. I feel like I definitely put up with a whole lot that I shouldn't have, but I didn't know what to do about it, except pray about everything. In hopes that Father God would work on my husband, I was always believing and hoping for miracles in my marriage, and I never ever seemed to give up.

In the fall of 2015, someone was killed, shot to death in the middle of the night on my front lawn. I woke up, because I saw lights real bright flashing. So I got up and looked out my window, only to see that the police lined up all around my house and neighborhood. It was so scary, being alone there with just me and my kids. I stuck it out in that house on the east side of Flint, Michigan, for a little over a year by myself with four kids. There was always gun shots you could hear in the neighborhood.

I wrote this book to tell one of my personal testimonies for Father God's kingdom.

A personal testimony about how Father God walked one Christian woman through a painful divorce.

Things my kids wrote to show their love to me:

Have a wonderful birthday!
Just like a star, I know you're there even when I don't see you.
Happy birthday, beautiful star, don't stop shining.

Dear Denise,
Years go by and time may fly, but no matter what, you'll always be in our hearts, and here is why. You're an amazing, beautiful woman, and we love you so much. Each day hard, not having you to spend it with, but you deserve to be happy.
Happy birthday to a wonderful daughter and mother.

With love,
Mom and kids

Wayne McGeathy

Nobody could have told me different about my ex-husband.

—Dee

Things my kids wrote to show their love to me:

> Who's the most beautiful woman on earth to me?
> My mom, Denise Dove. She's strong. She went
> through so much—divorce, court fighting, sup-
> porting me and my siblings. She's been through
> hell, but God was and is always there. She is one
> of the strongest women. I call my mom a soldier.
>   Even though she was broken, she stood tall,
> and no matter what, I'll defend her.
>   Good job, Mom, keep up the fight.
>   I love ya.
>
> Your son,
Matt
>
> P.S. I'll never forget going through McDonald's
> and laughing for nothing, just because she was
> happy. I always think of the memory when I'm
> at work.
>   One hundred percent heart strong.

Matthew Watson
July 28, 2017

You can't help them fully climb over the mountain, until your journey has taken you there already.

—A friend

Things my kids wrote to show their love to me:

Happy Mother's Day, Mom. I love you so much, and I am so thankful for you to be my mother. You are amazing and gorgeous! And the best Mom ever! You put up with my attitude, and when I'm being disrespectful. But no matter what, you're always there by my side.

Mom, I don't know how to explain it, but you're my mother. We have our ups and downs, but at the end, we are here together. I love you to the moon and back. Honestly, I would be lost without you! You make me smile every day, even if I am in a bad mood.

I will always be there for you, Mom, no matter what, because I love you! You're my world and my joy! I hate seeing you depressed and hurt, because you're my other half. But, Mom, I am so happy that you got over what happened recently.

You are a strong woman, a gorgeous one too! You are amazing. People say things, but yet, they're dumb. They obviously don't know you're good enough. But I'm always gonna be here for you! If you're hurt, I'm hurt. If you're happy, I'm happy; your feelings are mine. I obviously wouldn't know what to do without you.

Thank you so much, Mom.
Liliana Faith Dove
May 2015

You keep track of all my sorrows. You have collected all my tears in your bottle. You have recorded each one in your book.

—Psalm 56:8, NLT

Expressing the Hurt

One morning, I woke up, my family is together—laughing, drinking coffee. My dad and mom was in love. Then, I woke up another morning, my dad's gone, my mom's crying. What happened? He left my mom. Then, when I thought it couldn't get worse, it did. My family fell apart. I have never felt more pain than this. I wish it could be fixed, but it can't. I hate it.

I just wanna feel love. I can't, all I feel is pain. It sucks to wake up and walk into no family. It hurts to know you only got one. . .and I lost it.

I'll never forget when it all began.

Matt

Matthew Watson
September 11, 2017

It seemed like a "mockery," what happened to me through the divorce.

—Dee

CHAPTER SEVEN

Pain Amplified

What went on with me and my kids, and recent events, has been a whole new level of pain. Never in my wildest dreams ever thought the pain would be so intense. But it was so much more painful than I have been through in my past situations. It is hard for some other people to understand or relate to mine and my children's pain.

Especially, if they haven't gone through something similar. Me and my children have gone through a whole lot of grief, which shouldn't have surprised me, but yet, I guess I'd have to say that the intensity of the grieving process did, in fact, surprise me. I had come to the realization that "It is only Father God who can totally heal me." I regained my self-esteem and self-worth at the end of it all—my God—self-esteem. I started to pick myself up, started wearing make-up again, more, dressing nice again. I felt good enough about myself, in fact, to even enroll myself in medical college.

Also, my God-fearing man, who loves Jesus for real, genuinely loves Jesus and loves me and my children; he found me on a Christian website. This God-sent man is definitely an angel in disguise, for sure. He rescued me in every way. I fell madly in love with him; we are now married. Now, everything didn't turn out perfect the way I imagined it to, and my goal of having a little family again—the happily ever after little family—that I believed that Father God was going to restore in my life. But I realized, even if things didn't turn out how I intended or planned, the reality that things fell apart more and more, the harder I tried to hold things together, being "the pillar" in life that everyone always said I was when it came to my little family.

I know one thing for sure, I will never give up. Never give up hope that, one day, Father God will restore everything that the devil made sure was stripped from me and my children. I loved having a lot of children that I never would have dreamed of even having that many children though. When I was a young teenage girl, everyone that knew me even said that they couldn't picture me having a family. I guess it was because I waited longer to have a child than most other people did. But I had dreams of, one day, marrying and having a family, someday. I would always talk to my mother about it while I was growing up. It was just that I had big plans and goals for my life, even at a very young, tender age. When I was just a very young, little girl, I dreamed of being like Lorretta Lynn, singing songs and having a bunch of kids with the beautiful house, loving hubby; having all of it because of my success, I was going to have like Lorretta Lynn did in the "country music" scene. Wow, I sure did have big goals and dreams and big visions of when I grew up, of how my life was going to be. In fact, I started to dream of my life becoming amazing like Lorretta Lynn, who I looked up to as a little girl, when I was only seven. People in my family would ask me what I wanted to be when I grew up, and I would tell them, "I'm going to be a country music singer."

I kept that dream alive and did things to pursue it, until around 2004, when I was thirty-one years old. When I was only seven years of age, I dreamed of, one day, being a country music singer.

Once I married my now ex-husband and had all the children and all the load of a hard life on me, I gave up that dream a little bit more each time. For a while, I didn't give up, though. I mean I was in local contests in country music's radio stations all around the Genesee County area in Michigan.

And I remember in 2003, I won seventh place at one of the local bars that the contest was at. I sang a song by Loretta Lynn called "You're Not Woman Enough to Take My Man." I had a few people tell me that I shouldn't give up on singing, though. Also, I used to be in a choir at church and two praise bands—one at the church I attended, and the other praise band was at my huge "Celebrate Recovery" meeting that me and the kids went to on Friday nights in Flint, Michigan. The best place to be on a Friday night! One thing's for sure, I sure do want to get back into all of the singing for the Lord, and use my gifts again that He blessed me with. I hate being on a "back burner," being dormant, or on a book shelf, like this one lady had said to me at the altar, when I went up for prayer at my church one time. She, I guess, figured since I had all of those children that I had no business of being in ministry right then; she said that God had me on a book shelf for now.

Well, let me just say that I don't believe that Father God is going to put me on a book shelf so that I can get all dusty and waste time not doing the work of the ministry of reaching the lost/unsaved souls, whose lives are indeed in the balance of heaven or hell. I feel that Satan had lied to me enough, with me not flowing in the gifts that Father God gave me to use for the advancement of the kingdom of God. The devil had people, even if it was in the church, to discourage me, because he must have thought that I was a threat to his kingdom of darkness. That also, I would be helping pull people out of the kingdom of darkness with the power of the Holy Ghost living on the inside of me, because, the greater One lives in me, and He is all-powerful!

There was a lot of physical abuse with the children, mainly the older kids. Our son, Matt, was kicked on the head. My mother saw this in 2011. Then, when we lived in Creekwood, he ended up choking Matt, slamming him on the top of our van, because Matt raised his fist to me. Matt didn't want to go to church that Sunday on Mother's Day. My son was a good kid, and still is, it is just he had went through a lot in his young life. He's such a great kid with loads of gifts and talents. In fact, when he was just five years old, his teachers in kindergarten used to call him their "little preacher boy," because he would go to school and tell his classmates that if they didn't get saved by Jesus, they were going to go to hell. I was so surprised when they told me that! *Wow*, I thought, *my little preacher boy!*

The last incident that I remember happening was on the east side of Flint, Michigan.

All four of our children were in the living room when he dragged our daughter, Lily, by her hair and slapped her hard with his hands on her head. I was seating in the kitchen when I saw him do that to her, because she was getting mouthy with him. So I spoke up and said, "That's enough"!

I believe that I was intimidated by him big time. My oldest son, Wayne, did remember him manhandling me, he said. I didn't think I could do anything much, because he was my husband. The way I looked at it, is I needed to submit to my husband as unto the Lord. But I failed to realize that I was wrong about letting him have his way about everything. Because Father God wanted me to submit to my own husband as unto the Lord, but Father God did not want me to let him abuse the children.

I found out that there were many women out there that are *hiding* behind these abusive men. Because for one, many of us are scared, intimidated, hopeless, full of fear, not knowing what to really do about it. And if we are Christian women, then we get a little off balance with the "submitting to our husband's" part in the Bible! Or at least I did. I can really only speak for myself here as a Christian woman. Father God never expected me to stand back and watch my husband abuse our children.

Wives, submit yourselves to your own husbands, as you do to the Lord. For the husband is the head of the wife as Christ is the head of the church, His body, of which He is the Savior. Now as the church submits to their husbands in everything.

Husbands, love your wives, just as Christ loved the church and gave Himself up for her to make her holy, cleansing her by washing with water through the Word and to present her to Himself as a radiant church, without stain or wrinkle or any other blemish but holy and blameless. In the same way, husbands ought to love their wives as their own bodies. He who loves his wife loves himself.

After all, no one ever hated their body, but they feed and care for their body, just as Christ does the church—for we are members of His body. For this reason, a man will leave his father and mother and be united to his wife, and the two will become one flesh.

This is a profound mystery, but I am talking about Christ and the church. However, each one of you also must love his wife as he loves himself, and the wife must respect her husband. (Ephesians 5:22–33)

Adultery

You have heard that it was said, "You shall not commit adultery. But I tell you that anyone who looks at a woman lustfully has already committed adultery with her in his heart. If your right eye causes you to stumble, gouge it out and throw it away. It is better for you to lose one part of your body than for your whole body to be thrown into hell. And, if your right hand causes you to stumble, cut it off and throw it away. It is better for you to lose one part of your body, than for your whole body to go into hell."

Divorce

It has been said, "Anyone who divorces his wife must give her a certificate of divorce. But, I tell you that anyone who divorces his wife, except for sexual immorality, makes her the victim of adultery, and anyone who marries a divorce woman commits adultery." (Matthew 5:27–32)

In your anger do not sin. Do not let the sun go down while you are still angry. (Ephesians 4:26)

For this reason a man will leave his father and mother and be united to his wife, and the two will become one flesh? (Matthew 19:5)

That is why I heard it is so painful, because it's "a ripping away of the flesh."

For out of the heart come evil thoughts—murder, adultery, sexual immorality, theft, false testimony, slander. (Matthew 15:19)

Instead of your shame, you shall have double honor. (Isaiah 61:7)

"My divorce I had does not define me, it's something that happened to me" (Dee).

What is mankind that you are mindful of them, human beings that you care for them? You have made them a little lower than the angels and crowned them with glory and honor. (Psalm 8:4–5)

"The way I thought and believed was, 'I'm a Christian woman, divorce is not supposed to happen to me'" (Dee).

"The divorce had left me fragmented, with my only hope for full healing was I found out going to be through Christ alone" (Dee).

> The thief comes only to steal and kill and destroy; I have come that they may have life, and have it to the full. (John 10:10, NIV)

> To provide for those who grieve in Zion—to bestow on them a crown of beauty instead of ashes, the oil of joy instead of mourning, and a garment of praise instead of a spirit of despair. They will be called oaks of righteousness, a planting of the Lord for the display of His splendor. (Isaiah 61:3)

"My mom said to me after my divorce was over, 'You just wanted a husband'" (Dee).

> My dear children, I write this to you so that you will not sin. But, if anybody does sin, we have an advocate with the Father, Jesus Christ, the Righteous One. (1 John 2:1)

"I discovered after the divorce that I was glad that I was no longer the "run-down housewife no longer" (Dee).

> I praise You, because I am fearfully and wonderfully made; Your works are wonderful, I know that full well. (Psalm 139:14)

You intended to harm me, but God intended it
for good to accomplish what is now being done,
the saving of many lives. (Genesis 50:20)

All things are possible with God. (Matthew
19:26)

You shall not commit adultery. (Exodus 20:14)

Father God helped me accomplish a whole lot recently. He
helped me go and face a divorce. A divorce I never expected to have,
or never desired to have at first, until I learned the truth about what
my ex-husband was doing. And, until I was forced really to face and
look at the reality of me wanting to hold my marriage together, but
the reality of learning the hard way that he, however, did not want
to hold the marriage together. Because after all, he found for himself
or so he believed that the grass was greener on the other side of the
fence, or should I dare say, "The other side of the boarder?" But he
had failed to realize that, no matter what woman he was with, the
grass still needs to be watered and tended to.

The divorce was final on February 29, 2016, a leap year! I leaped
myself right out of that abusive marriage with Father God's help that
year! Kind of humorous when I put it that way, I guess. I graduated
the college I started in September 2015, graduation date was May 6,
2016. Then, I proceeded to move on with my life, move forward all
the way and moved to Connecticut in June of 2016. Me and Rob
were married on October 22, 2017, which, after having the abusive
marriage I had, was nothing but "a miracle marriage," a true blessing
from Father God. I didn't expect actually to be getting married again,
especially after the marriage Father God helped release me from.

But Father God is so very good and faithful, even when no
one else seems to be faithful in our lives. Father God proves to be
faithful, at least to me, in my life over and over again! He truly is
a miracle-working God! In my much younger years, I picked out a
man I thought would be a good husband, maybe even a "godly man."
But later get blown off my feet by Father God when He picks out a

man He intends for me to have in my life, instead of who I thought was going to be a good, godly husband. I admit Father God sure does have way better taste in picking out a man that would make a good husband than I did, by far! And I am eternally and forever grateful to Father God!

Wish I could say I've had an easy road when first moving to Connecticut to start the new life Father God had given to me and my children, but I didn't. I came up to a dead end, as I tried to pursue a job in my new field of work as a medical assistant, for months on end trying. It sure wasn't as easy as I set out for it to be, and believe me, I was persistent. It didn't seem to matter though, interview after interview, months on end, doors slammed shut as opportunities that I believed and thought and extremely had hope for didn't happen. It didn't work out for this eager, strong woman of God, now single mother of only two young children I had with me at that time, under the age of six.

I didn't want to crawl back defeated to my home state of Michigan either. I had it in my mind that I and my two children were going to make it. Me and those two kids were going to make it in the new life I was believing God to restore unto us. But when it didn't turn out just like that, I admit it, I got really scared. I was scared of me becoming homeless with those two precious gifts that Father God had blessed me with. I may have been dealing with a little bit of pride there, ego even, as a woman, as strong woman of faith.

I wasn't going to let the devil win, I thought though, *what was I going to do?* I even asked for help from the welfare system, which I felt ashamed of asking. I felt embarrassed, humiliated to say the least, belittled as a "single parent." That didn't seem to work out in my favor fast enough, either. So soon I ended up not having enough income. And, soon the sheriff of my town showed up to my little cottage house with an eviction. This was absolutely horrible. I ended up contacting several agencies in the area to see if I could possibly find some help. But, once again, there I was, defeated, hopeless, and to no avail, I was evicted. I felt like a failure deep inside, like I let those two babies down.

What I felt even more shameful and embarrassed is that this wasn't my first eviction, either. After my ex-husband pulled the lovely stunt he pulled of abandoning me and all four of his children on the east side of Flint, Michigan, I held the fort for a little over a year, which was nothing short of a miracle in itself that I was able to sustain us as long as I did with Father God's help, of course. Because, we can do absolutely nothing without Father God helping us.

I ended up having to stay a little while with my blind disabled mother and oldest son, Wayne, in Michigan, which I felt that I was such a burden to their household with me and all my children. I knew when I asked my mother to stay there with her and my oldest son, Wayne, it would be just temporary, anyways. I ended up staying there for about a month with my four children. The way I looked at it was, we were also spending quality time with my mother and the children's grandmother. So, when we were there, I helped out any way I could by cleaning the house and cooking meals and running errands for them.

I set out to Connecticut, with just my two youngest kids. The older kids wanted to stay behind in Michigan. So I figured they were old enough to make that decision, the three older kids. It was an extremely long drive by myself with just me and two little kids. I had to stop, obviously, several times for potty breaks, to eat and to put my three-year old daughter's seat belt back on in her car seat, because she got restless on such a long trip, which was completely normal for a tiny little child like her, anyways. I knew it was going to be like that though, in fact, I talked about it—the trip, how it was going to be for the babies with my sister in Louisiana.

From the hood to Connecticut.

—Dee

Whelp, it's always been said about me, and I believe it to be true! That when I set out to do something, I go and do it! But, I had a real hard time finding a place to rent at first. We spent three days about in my truck, which I knew wasn't good. Then, I ended up deciding on camping at a camp ground in a tent for three weeks. I went shopping at Walmart with the kids to buy food, camping gear, and a tent. We had a fun time together camping. We had bonfires most every night, s'mores, hot dogs over the bonfire, grilled out on a portable grill that was given to me from another camper, and just had "bonding" moments that could never be replaced or forgotten. There was a playground, showers—it was actually a special time.

Then, after three weeks of looking like a mad woman, an affordable place to rent I heard about—a little cottage that was for rent just a ways down the road in a nearby little town. It has a two-bedroom, it had a good size yard and was in walking distance to nearby beaches, which on real hot days, I walked down to with my youngest child in a stroller. We stayed in that cottage from July to November 2016, but I ended up taking the two little ones to Michigan to stay with my brother's fiancée in October. I figured, until I had gotten stable on my feet.

I had gotten scared that I was going to end up homeless with my two young children. So I ended up having to make one of the hardest decisions a mother could ever make, by taking to stay with relatives. Well, I didn't get on my feet fast enough, the state of Michigan stepped in and took my kids from where I had placed them at, because they said that there was allegations of abuse at my brother's fiancées house.

So in February 2017, the CPS of Michigan gave the two little ones over to their dad. They wanted me to come, but I had no money and no vehicle that would, at the time, make it all the way back to Michigan. So there I was, once again, feeling like a failure, hopeless, defeated, and weak. I felt like I let my children down. So, as of now, the two youngest kids are with their dad and his new wife in Canada.

Sure wish this was a happy ending, where me and my new husband were raising my kids together, but it's not, at least not right now. Maybe Father God has a miracle for us in the future though, who knows, but Father God knows. Absolutely nothing takes Father God by surprise. So, yes, my heart is still in a whole lot of pain. I can only imagine my two younger children's emotions and feelings. They are too young to understand.

When my ex-husband ended up taking the two younger children, I said to him, "Haven't you done enough? Haven't you caused enough pain?" It seems that me and the kids have to suffer because of the situation that he helped cause. I've said to many people that the divorce was a "domino effect," a chain of events.

My ex-husband's new wife contacted me on a text message, since I been in Connecticut. She wanted to ask me if I thought he had cheated on her. I wanted so bad to say, "Yes, I believe he has cheated on you, because he's never been faithful to any women he's ever been with." He'd fooled around with many, many other women ever since I've known him, since I was just fifteen when I met him at a roller rink. He never changed, like I always hoped and prayed for him to change, but it never happened.

I looked at it this way though: "It's not my business or my problem." I wasn't going to have them drag me into that drama. I was way smarter than that. I figured it was now her baby, she can rock it. Also, after all, she wanted a married man with a bunch of kids, so she got exactly what she wanted. Besides, I wasn't going to let the devil use them to play mind games with my emotions ever again.

Can't wait to see the fruit of all the pain and suffering from my past testimonies help others heal and come through too.

—Dee

They triumphed over him by the blood of the Lamb and the word of their testimony; they did not love their lives so much to shrink from death. (Revelation 12:11)

After a while, it seems that I beat myself up saying to myself, *Why did I have to marry that man!* I felt stupid as a woman, being so blind to all the years of infidelity, not wanting to believe or see it. Because I was so used to seeing the best in everyone and also being the (big faith) woman, believing that God was someday going to change my spouse, which there is nothing wrong with believing God to change and heal marriages. But some marriages don't find healing and restoration, because everyone has a "free will."

But the person who really ended up changing was myself. The way I figured it is, if I spoke God's Word over him and prayed until I was "blue in the face," then a (big) miracle was going to happen. Because after all, "the God I served was definitely a miracle working God who parted the red sea" (Exodus 14:21); "turned water into wine" (John 2:1–11); "all things are possible with God" (Matthew 19:26).

Although, those things are very true, I forgot to realize that everyone has a free will. Father God is a true gentleman. He doesn't force anyone to follow or serve Him. None of us are robots. We all have choices in this life. One of my dreams and desires of my heart was to have my own family. It was so very excruciatingly painful to see my kids and everything I fought so hard to hold everything together to be torn to sherds by the enemy (the devil). I hated so much to see the pain and disbelief it caused my children. Again, I was so in disbelief and shock that I thought to myself, *Why or how could this be happening to me—I am a Christian woman who loves God and her family.*

The question I should have thought was, "Why not me?" Because I learned as a Christian from the enemy attacking me and my family. Also, I had Christian friends all over the country and world praying too. Not all divorces are the same, as I learned going through my divorce, God sometimes will heal a marriage, and other times, He will pull you out of that marriage, if the spouse is abusive and is not willing to submit to God.

I know what it feels like to be shaken on the inside. I have had it happen in 2006, when the infidelity was first noticed. Then again, it happened in February 2015, which I was so shocked that he would do it again after everything. For me, the divorce I found has been more painful than a death, from my viewpoint. I have learned the best way to get through a divorce is to allow yourself a permission to feel the pain and all the emotions. But then, keep turning them over to the care of Father God. The darkness that was all around me seemed to grip me at times. During my divorce, I would look up my staircase and cry and say, "Jesus, please help me."

> Cast your cares on the Lord, and He will sustain you; He will never let the righteous be shaken (Psalm 55:22).

Since I been in Connecticut, I had a neighbor friend who had to take me to the airport and drop me off when my brother, Doug, unexpectedly and suddenly died in Michigan.

As he was driving me to the airport, he talked to me. When he found out that I moved to Connecticut before, never been here ever, he said, "Wow, that takes some guts to do that."

I told him that it takes faith in God, and that I moved before to Tulsa, Oklahoma, without really knowing exactly where me and my ex-husband were going, went there also by faith alone. I know when people here have talked to me, here in Connecticut, it usually, I guess, pretty much blows their minds when they learn that about me. But I walk by faith and not by sight.

> For we walk by faith, not by sight. (2 Corinthians 5:7, KJV)

> But without faith it is impossible to please Him: for he that cometh to God must believe that He is a rewarder of them that diligently seek Him. (Hebrews 11:6, KJV)

> Now the just shall live by faith: but if any man draw back, My soul shall have no pleasure in him. (Hebrews 10:38, KJV)

Just want to say that this book was written not to discourage people from getting married and having a family. Or to say, that Father God doesn't still heal marriages. Because He, in fact, does. He is the same God yesterday, today, and forever (Hebrews 13:8).

> They triumphed over him by the blood of the Lamb and by the word of their testimony; they did not love their lives so much to shrink from death. (Revelation 12:11, NIV)

This book was also written to just tell my testimony (my story) of how I stayed strong during the most painful time in mine and my children's life. It's about moving forward in life in spite of all the anguishing pain, disappointment, fear, tears upon tears, moving forward for a greater purpose. I am still believing that, one day, Father God will restore my children to me, in my life, so I haven't given up hope, because after all, I have the God, of all hope, in my life. As long as I have Jesus in my life, as my Lord and personal savior, I always will have hope. Also, I just want to thank all the many friends and families who supported me and my children with your many prayers and love during one of the very hardest and most painful time of our lives. Please do continue to pray for me and my children, because the enemy is constantly coming at us, especially, a family who has ministry callings on their lives, and thank you all, so very much, from the very bottom of our hearts. Also, if you all ever need me and my husband, Rob, to ever hold you or your families up in prayer, please do not hesitate to contact us, because the body of Christ needs one another. We weren't meant to walk this life alone.

So, if you are going through something similar, don't give up hope. Just because my situation was not like I hoped, it did turn out, for the most part, how I hoped. It just ripped out my heart to not have my children with me. My husband now, Rob, is what I always dreamed of having—a God-fearing husband. Just for now, minus my beautiful kids, so yes, I am still broken right now, in a lot of ways. But because of my personal relationship with Jesus Christ, "I'm broken but beautiful."

Much love, all prayers.

Love,
Denise

The man who hates and divorces his wife, says the Lord, the God of Israel, "Does violence to the one he should protect," says the Lord Almighty. So, be on your guard, and do not be unfaithful. (Malachi 2:16)

Our very first pic together, Rob & Dee
"July 2016" "Nantic, Connecticut"

Rob & Dee
"Summer of 2018" Groton Connecticut

Denise
Mystic Connecticut "Sept. 2018"

Me & Rob
"Sept. 2018" Mystic Connecticut

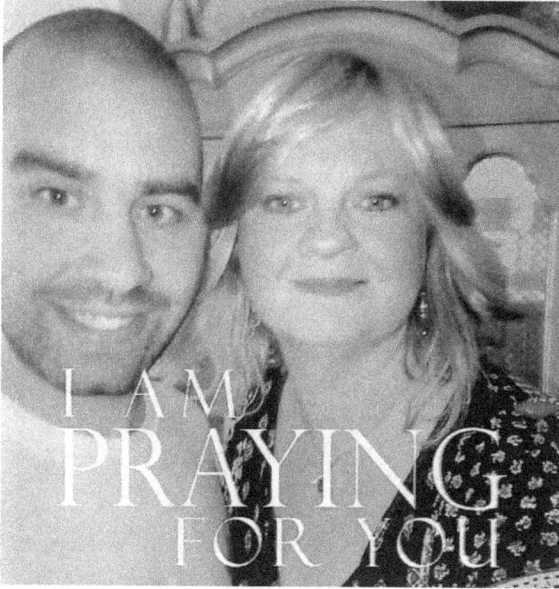

Me & Rob
"Our first apartment"
"New London, Connecticut" "2017"

Me & Rob
"Our first apartment"
"New London, Connecticut" "2017"

Me & Rob
"October 22, 2018"
"Our very first wedding anniversary pics"

Me & Rob
Our first apartment
"New London, Connecticut" "2017"

Me & Rob
Our first apartment
"New London, Connecticut" "2017"

Me & Rob
"Mystic Connecticut" "Sept. 2018"

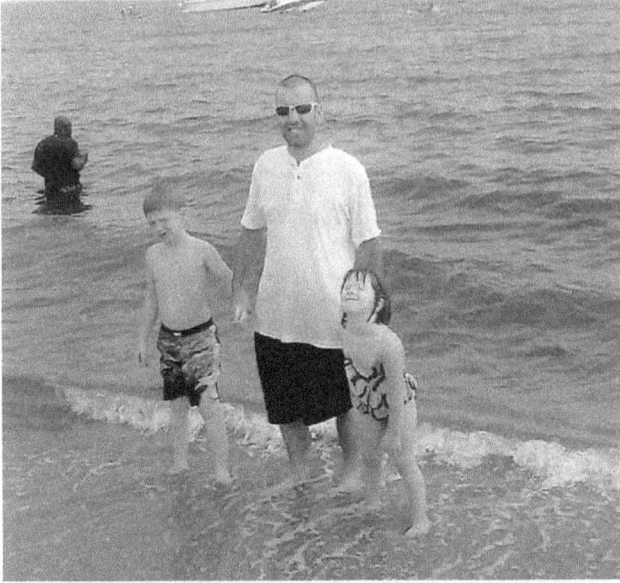

Rob & Luke & Heaven in Niantic, Connecticut "2016"

My mom "Mary Jane" & my Dad "Henry" "1970"

Left to Right
My Dad Henry, brother Wayne, sister Kim, my Mom
"Mary Jane", me the baby, & brother Doug "1975"

Me with my very first granddaughter "Alanah"
January 13, 2019

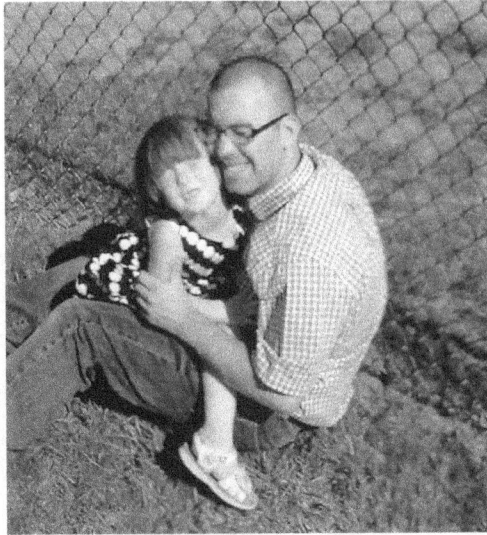

Rob & Heaven
Old Lyme Connecticut "2016"

Especially Sweet

Rob & Denise
The day we got married "October 22, 2017"

Rob & Dee
The day we got married "October 22, 2017"

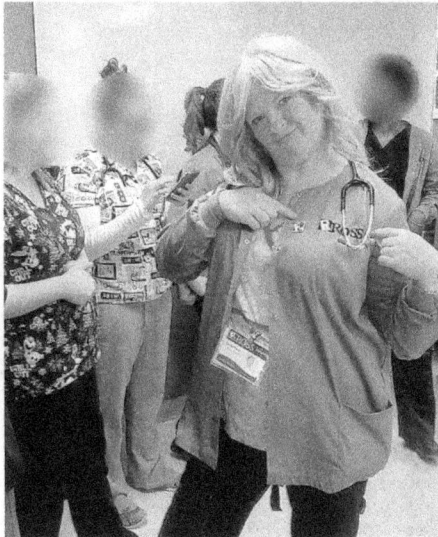

Flint, Michigan "2016"
Dee

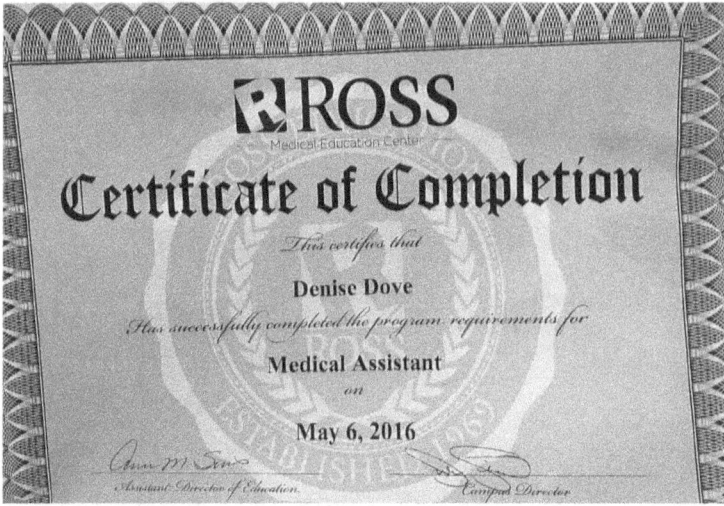

Dee & Big brother Doug "1999"

Dee, son Luke & daughter Liliana
Burton, Michigan "2013"

My book was written in the year of "2017"

Denise in Mystic Connecticut
"October 22, 2018"

Rob & Dee at the "Joyce Meyer confrence in mass" "2018"

Rob & Dee in Niantic, Connecticut summer of "2017"

Burton, Michigan "2017"
Second to oldest son Matthew

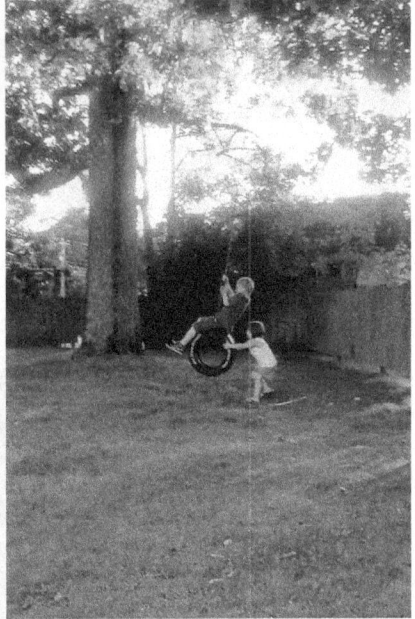

Luke & Heaven at my calien house I rented
in Old Lyme, Connecticut "2016"

Flint Michigan "2015
My son Matthew and Dee

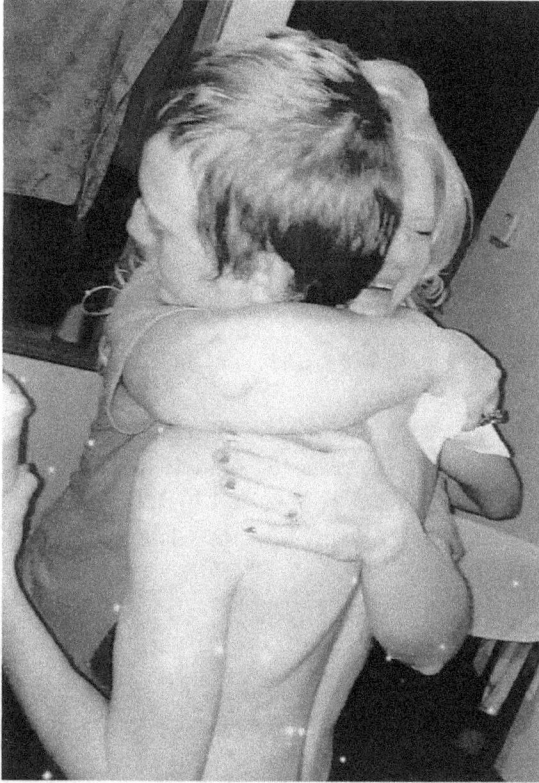

October 2017 my mom's house in Burton, Michigan
Dee & son Matthew

After I gotten to Michigan for my brother
Doug's funeral when I first saw him

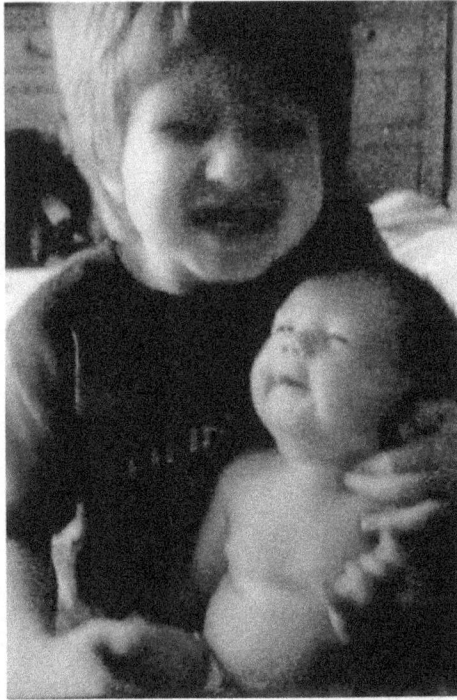

Luke & Heaven "2012"
My house in "Burton, Michigan"

Wayne, Liliana, Matthew & Luke
"December 2017" My mom's house in Burton, Michigan

"Easter 2016"
Dee with Heaven & Luke
My mom's house in Burton, Michigan

House on the East side of Flint, Michigan
Last Christmas I had together with all of my kids, "Christmas 2015"
"Heaven"

October "2012"
Me, son Matthew behind me, Liliana holding
Heaven & me holding Luke
Holly, Michigan, Seven Lakes State Park

On left daughter Liliana & Me
"April 2018" "New London Connecticut, Ocean Beach"

Dee & Daughter Lilian
"April 2018" "New London, Connecticut"

Rob, Denise & Daughter Liliana
"April 2018"

Daughter Liliana, Denise & Rob
"April 2018"

Denise & daughter Liliana
"April 2018"

Dee
Ocean Beach New London, Connecticut "April 2018"

Flint, Michigan
Dee & son Luke on his fifth birthday "2014"

Brother Doug behind brotherWayne
brother Doug by himself

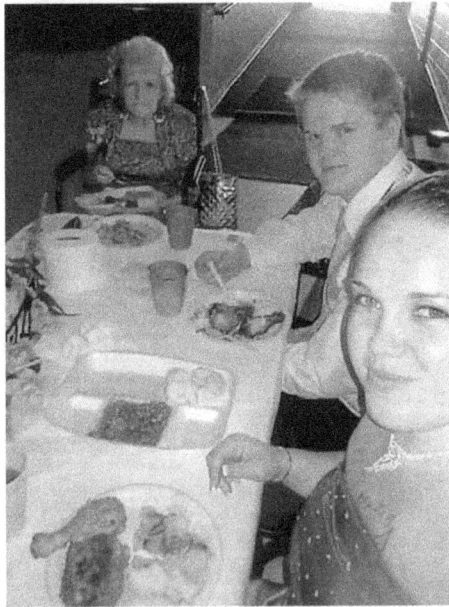

My mom, son Wayne & niece Steph
"Renewal of vow wedding August 17, 2013"

Me & my mom at "Renewal of vows wedding"
"August 17, 2013"

Dee & niece Steph
August 17, 2013

Dee & the two youngest Luke & Heaven
August 17, 2013

Dee & Bride maids
August 17, 2013

Second oldest son Matthew
August 17, 2013

My mom MaryJane at my "Renewal of vows wedding"
August 17, 2013

Dee & oldest son Wayne
August 17, 2013

Dee
August 17, 2013

Dee with daughter Heaven
"August 17, 2013"

Me & Rob
"October 22, 2018"
"Our very first wedding anniversary pics"

Me & Rob
"October 22, 2018"
"Our very first wedding anniversary pics"

Dee
"2018"

Me & Rob
"October 22, 2018"
"Our very first wedding anniversary pics"

Me & Rob
"October 22, 2018"
"Our very first wedding anniversary pics"

All five of my kids the day "Heaven Glory" was
born at the hospital "August 30, 2012"

My mom "Mary Jane" memorial shadow box I made
"2019"

Memorial I made of my mom "Mary Jane"
"2019

My brother Doug's memorial shadow box I made
"2019"

My brother Wayne's memorial shadow box I made
"2019"

Me with Luke & Heaven
"Niantic, Connecticut" "2016"

Luke on the beach
"Niantic, Connecticut, 2016"

Heaven getting ready for the beach
"2016"

Me & my son Luke
"mommy & son dance, 2016"

Me & Wayne
"October 2017" "Burton, Michigan"

Me in Mystic, Connecticut
"October 22, 2018"

Flint, Michigan
Me & daughter Heaven, my youngest
"January 13, 2019"

I cried when I seen them, "January 13, 2019"
Flint, Michigan at the hospital when daughter
Lilian gave birth to Alanah

"January 13, 2019"
Me, Luke & Heaven

"January 13, 2019"
Me, Wayne, Luke & Heaven

ABOUT THE AUTHOR

Denise Dove-Bernier was born and raised on the south side of Flint, Michigan. She is a very proud mother of five beautiful talented children who are gifts from Father God. Denise graduated from Davison High School in Davison, Michigan. She went to Mott Community College and also graduated from Ross Medical Education as a medical assistant. She loves cooking and baking, going for romantic walks with her husband, Bible studying, being spontaneous in life, loves going to the beach, loves music, singing, and is an evangelist of Broken But Beautiful Ministries, which she started by faith. Denise has a huge heart to reach the lost, those who don't have a personal relationship with Jesus Christ.

Denise resides in Mystic, Connecticut, where she and her husband, Rob, have an online live ministry video on Facebook. She is newly, very happily married.

Denise and her husband, Rob, have become licensed and ordinated on May 6, 2019.

Printed in the USA
CPSIA information can be obtained
at www.ICGtesting.com
LVHW051529230224
772661LV00001B/167

9 781645 849100